The Story of a Special Day
Volume 257

September 13

The 256th day of the year (257th in leap years). There are 109 days remaining until the end of the year.

by Michael Dobson

Timespinner
Press

This book is also available in e-book form for Kindle, e-pub devices, and other formats from your favorite online booksellers.

For more information about the series, about us, or about your special day, please email us at editor@timespinnerpress.com.

Look for other volumes in *The Story of a Special Day*, coming often. See www.timespinnerpress.com for details and for the most recent information.

Table of Contents

Cover: Michelangelo's *David* (Photo: Jörg Bittner Unna, CC BY-SA 3.0). Michelangelo began carving this statue on September 13, 1501 — the **Cover Story.**

Quote of the Day

"If we believe in the existence of a great moral and political evil amongst us, and that duty, honour, and interest, call upon us to prepare the way for its removal, we must act."

Francis Scott Key, author of "The Star-Spangled Banner." The banner that inspired Key flew over Ft. McHenry on the night of September 13, 1814

Today
in
History

September 13

September, from the Brevarium Grimani

What Happened on September 13?

While some days of the year are more famous than others, every day of the year is filled with important, exciting, and unusual events, from religious awakenings to natural disasters, from wars to breakthroughs in technology, and from tragedy to triumph.

In this section, you'll learn about all the events that make September 13 important, including the special event that makes up our cover story or event of the day. Some events you may already know about, others may be new to you, but all of them are important parts of the history of the work.

Let's explore some of the reasons why September 13 is a very special day!

David at the Galleria dell'Accademia, showing its relative size. (Photo: Korido, CC BY-SA 4.0)

Cover Story
Michelangelo Sculpts David (1501)

Michelangelo, generally considered one of the greatest artists of all time, lived in the Republic of Florence during the High Renaissance period (1490s to 1527). A contemporary (and rival) of Leonardo da Vinci, Michelangelo produced masterpieces of sculpture, painting, and architecture, with two of his most famous pieces, the *Pietà* and *David,* completed before Michelangelo reached the age of 30.

The massive statue of David stands 17 feet (5.2 meters) high, and today can be seen in the Galleria dell'Accademia in Florence. It is considered one of the greatest sculptures ever created. *David* was encased in brick during World War II to protect it from bombs. It was damaged by a man with a hammer in 1991, and has undergone some restoration because of deterioration of the marble.

David happened almost by accident. On his return to Florence after several years living in Rome, he was asked to complete an unfinished statue of David that had been abandoned more than forty years ago. Michelangelo convinced the sponsors to give him the commission (beating out da Vinci), and began carving the statue on September 13, 1501. It took him a little over two years to complete the massive sculpture.

Although it was originally seen as a Biblical sculpture, it became a symbol of Florentine independence. David's eyes, filled warning, were turned toward Rome.

Event of the Day
The Star-Spangled Banner Flies (1814)

During the War of 1812, Francis Scott Key, a young lawyer, set sail from Baltimore Harbor, flying a flag of truce authorized by US President James Madison. Along with his colleague John Stuart Skinner, Key's mission was to negotiate an exchange of prisoners with the British.

On September 7, 1814, the two men boarded the British flagship, HMS *Tonnant*, and dined with British Major General Robert Ross and Vice Admiral Alexander Cochrane. The negotiation was difficult, but finally Key and Skinner obtained the agreement. In the process, however, the two Americans heard details of the British plan to attack Baltimore. As a result, they were held captive by the British until after the attack.

The Battle of Baltimore began on September 12 when the British landed 4,000 troops at North Point, Maryland, who were met by 3,200 Americans. Ultimately, the US forces retreated, but only after inflicting heavy casualties on the attacking British, including General Ross.

The British attacked again the next day, but the American had time to prepare. Over 100 cannons and 10,000 troops faced 4,300 British attackers. Realizing they could not prevail, the British elected to bombard Fort McHenry, which guarded the entrance to Baltimore Harbor. That night, September 13, a British fleet consisting of nineteen ships began attacking with Congreve rockets and mortar shells.

By Dawn's Early Light, Edward Percy Moran. Francis Scott Key is standing, with arm outstretched toward the flag flying over Ft. McHenry

  Michael Dobson

The Star-Spangled Banner flag on display at the Smithsonian Institution's
National Museum of American History (Courtesy SIA)

Fort McHenry was defended by 1,000 soldiers commanded by Major George Armistead. Through the rainy night of September 13, Fort McHenry flew its storm flag.

Francis Scott Key watched the bombardment from aboard HMS *Tonnant*, but with the "rocket's red glare" and "bombs bursting in air," he could not see well enough to know how the battle turned out. The American victory was revealed at "dawn's early light," when the smaller storm flag was replaced by an oversized American flag created by Mary Pickersgill and her 13-year old daughter. A few British riflemen fired at the flag, but then retreated to the shoreline.

Inspired by what he'd seen, Key wrote a poem on the back of a letter he was carrying, and the next day at his hotel finished the poem, titled "Defence of Fort M'Henry." Key's brother-in-law realized the words of the poem fit the popular melody "To Anacreon in Heaven," and thus "The Star-Spangled Banner" was born, Originally one of several patriotic songs used in official ceremonies, it became the US National Anthem in 1931.

The flag itself, which measured 30 feet by 42 feet, deteriorated with continued use, and pieces of the flag were made into souvenirs and gifts. It was donated to the Smithsonian Institution in 1912, and was restored several times, the most recent a $21 million preservation effort completed in 2008. It remains on display at the Smithsonian's National Museum of American History in Washington, DC.

More September 13 Events

From the creation of great works of engineering and art, to devastating wars and natural disasters, thousands of years of history have left their mark on each and every day of the year. Here are some important events that occurred on September 13. (Illustrated items are shaded.)

1541 — French theologian and reformer **John Calvin** returns to Geneva, Switzerland, and begins his church reforms, known as **Calvinism**, foundation of Reformed, Presbyterian, and Congregationalist faith traditions.

John Calvin

1847 — During the **Mexican-American War,** nine teenage military cadets (known as the **Niños Héroes**) die while defending Chapultepec Castle from invading US forces. According to legend, Cadet Juan Escutia wrapped the Mexican flag around his body and jumped from the top of the castle to keep the flag from falling into enemy hands. *(See page 53.)*

The Military College of Chapultepec, where Los Niños Heroes studied
(Print: Currier & Ives, circa 1847)

1848 — American railroad construction worker Phineas P. Gage survives an accident in which a large iron rod is driven completely through his head (known as the "**American Crowbar Case**"). The effects of this injury on his personality and behavior had a major influence on 19th century scientific work on the nature of the mind and brain.

1862 — A Union Army corporal discovers **an envelope with three cigars and a copy of Robert E. Lee's plans** for the Maryland Campaign of the American Civil War, which plays a significant role in the Union response at the Battle of Antietam.

1889 — New Yorker Henry Bliss becomes the **first person killed by a motor vehicle crash** in the Western Hemisphere when he is struck by an electric-powered taxicab at West 74th Street and Central Park West. He dies of his injuries the following day.

1948 — **Margaret Chase Smith** becomes the **first woman** to serve in both the US **House** of Representatives and the **Senate**.

1962 — The US District Court enters an injunction to require the **University of Mississippi** to admit its first African-American student, **James Meredith**. The US government sends troops to enforce his admission, which took place October 1.

1971 — An **uprising at Attica Prison**, New York, ends when the state police retake the prison. A total of 43 people die.

1985 — The video game *Super Mario Brothers* is released in Japan.

Henry Bliss

Margaret Chase Smith

"Integration at Ole Miss" (Photo: Marion S. Trikosko, *US News & World Report*). **James Meredith** walks to class accompanied by US marshals.

Quote of the Day

"Although we talk so much about
coincidence we do not really believe in it.
In our heart of hearts we think better of the
universe, we are secretly convinced that it
is not such a slipshod, haphazard affair,
that everything in it has meaning."

J. B. Priestley, novelist and playwright
born September 13, 1894

Births
and
Deaths
THER
ACC
MAGNA
September 13

General John J. "Black Jack" Pershing, highest-ranking officer ever to serve in the US Army in his own lifetime. Pershing was born September 13, 1860. (Photo: George Grantham Bain)

Notable September 13 People

With the current world population at about seven billion people, on average about 19 million people also celebrate their birthdays on September 13 — and that isn't counting millions and millions who came before! No matter when you were born, you share your birthday with many special people whose accomplishments (and occasionally embarrassments) have been noted as part of history.

In this section, you'll meet fascinating people who share your birthday. They're organized by what they're famous for, and then in reverse chronological order from most recent to earliest. Those who are shown in photographs or artwork have a box around them. We don't have photos of everyone, so please forgive us if your favorite person is missing.

Some of these people you've heard of, others will be new to you, but they all make up an important part of the reason that September 13 is a truly special day!

Claudette Colbert, actress, born September 13, 1903

Who Was Born on September 13?

Art and Photography

Kevin Carter, South African photojournalist who received a Pulitzer Prize for his photograph of the 1993 Sudan famine; subject of the 2010 biopic *The Bang-Bang Club. (1908)*

Anne Geddes, known for her photographs of babies in such books as the New York Times best-selling *Down in the Garden. (1956)*

Robert Indiana, artist whose best known work is his graphic "LOVE." *(1928)*

Robert Indiana's LOVE graphic on a 1973 stamp

Business and Fashion

Stella McCartney, fashion designer and daughter of Beatle Paul McCartney. *(1971)*

Milton S. Hershey, founder of the Hershey Chocolate Company and the town of Hershey, Pennsylvania; noted philanthropist. *(1857)*

Milton S. Hershey

Entertainment

Robbie Kay, actor in *Pirates of the Caribbean: On Stranger Tides,* and the television series *Heroes Reborn* and *Once Upon a Time.* (1995)

Louise Lombard, actress known as Evangeline in the BBC series *The House of Eliott* and Sofia in the CBS series *CSI: Crime Scene Investigation*. *(1970)*

Tyler Perry, comedian, actor, and filmmaker known for the character of Madea, and for his television series including *Tyler Perry's House of Payne*. *(1969)*

Jean Smart, actress best known for playing Charlene on *Designing Women* and Lana on *Frasier*. *(1951)*

Nell Carter, actress and singer known for her role on the sitcom *Gimme a Break!* and the Broadway musical *Ain't Misbehavin'*. *(1948)*

Frank Marshall, film producer and director who co-founded Amblin Entertainment with Steven Spielberg and the Kennedy/Marshall Company with his wife and frequent collaborator Kathleen Kennedy. *(1946)*

Jacqueline Bisset, actress whose films include *Bullitt, Airport, Day for Night, Murder on the Orient Express,* and *The Deep*. *(1944)*

Don Bluth, animation director and producer whose best known films include *The Secret of NIMH, An American Tail, The Land Before Time, All Dogs Go to Heaven,* and *Anastasia*. *(1937)*

Eileen Fulton, actress best known for playing Lisa Grimaldi on *As the World Turns* between 1960 and 2010. *(1933)*

Barbara Bain, actress best known for her co-starring roles in the TV series *Mission: Impossible* and *Space: 1999. (1931)*

Barbara Bain with Alf Kjellin from *Mission: Impossible*

Reta Shaw, actress who played the cook in the film *Mary Poppins* and the housekeeper in the television series *The Ghost & Mrs. Muir. (1912)*

Mae Questel, actress and voice artist best known as the voice of the animated characters Betty Boop and Olive Oyl; played Aunt Bethany in *National Lampoon's Christmas Vacation. (1908)*

Reta Shaw (right) with Hermione Baddeley from *Mary Poppins*

Mae Questel

Claudette Colbert, Hollywood leading lady whose best known films include her Academy Award-winning role in *It Happened One Night* and the title role in the 1934 version of *Cleopatra*. (1903) *(Photo page 22.)*

Jesse L. Lasky, pioneering movie producer who founded what later became Paramount Studios. *(1880)*

Government and Politics

Óscar Arias, president of Costa Rica who won the 1987 Nobel Peace Prize for his efforts to end the Central American crisis. *(1940)*

Cesare Borgia, member of the famous Borgia family, known for intrigue and power in 15th century Italy. Illegitimate son of Pope Alexander VI and brother of Lucrezia Borgia; his fight for power is one of the major inspirations for Niccolo Machiavelli's *The Prince*. *(1475)*

Literature and Poetry

Mildred D. Taylor, won the Newbery Medal for her 1977 novel *Roll of Thunder, Hear My Cry*. *(1908)*

Else Holmelund Minarik, American children's book author best known for the *Little Bear* series. *(1920)*

Portrait of a Gentleman (Cesare Borgia), by Altobello Melone

Roald Dahl, British author whose best known works include the children's novels *Charlie and the Chocolate Factory* and *James and the Giant Peach*; also wrote macabre short stories for adults. He was a fighter ace with the RAF during World War II and later an intelligence officer. *(1916)*

Roald Dahl (right) with wife Patricia Neal (Photo: Carl Van Vechten)

J. B. Priestley, prolific English novelist and playwright, known for his social commentary. Best known works include the novel *The Good Companions*, the play *An Inspector Calls*, and the travelogue *English Journey. (1894)*

Sherwood Anderson, American novelist and short-story writer best known for his short-story cycle *Winesburg, Ohio,* ranked as one of the 100 best 20th century English-language novels. *(1876)*

Military and Command

Max Prüß, captain of the LZ129 *Hindenburg* zeppelin on its final voyage, which ended in disaster. Prüß survived the event. *(1891)*

Stanley Lord, captain of the SS *Californian,* which was in the vicinity of HMS *Titanic* the night of its sinking but did not come to *Titanic's* assistance. *(1877)*

John J. Pershing, commander of the American Expeditionary Force during World War I. Only American promoted in his lifetime to the rank of General of the Armies[*], sometimes called a "six-star general," though Pershing himself wore four gold stars rather than the traditional silver worn by other generals. *(1860) (Photo page 20.)*

Walter Reed, US Army physician who proved the link between mosquitos and yellow fever, enabling the Panama Canal to be completed. The Walter Reed National Military Medical Center is named for him. *(1851)*

---

[*] George Washington was given the same rank posthumously, on the theory that no serving US military officer should ever outrank George Washington.

Music

Fiona Apple, singer-songwriter who won a Grammy for "Criminal," from her debut album *Tidal.* *(1977)*

Zak Starkey, drummer with The Who and Oasis; son of Beatles drummer Ringo Starr. *(1965)*

Dave Mustaine, musician best known as co-founder of Megadeth and original lead guitarist of Metallica. *(1961)*

Joni Sledge, founding member of Sister Sledge, best known for their hit "We Are Family." *(1956)*

Don Was, musician and producer who led the 1980s band Was (Not Was). *(1952)*

Randy Jones, disco and pop singer best known as the cowboy in the Village People. *(1908)*

Peter Cetera, original member of the rock band Chicago; composed and sang their hit "If You Leave Me Now." Member of the Rock and Roll Hall of Fame and the Songwriters Hall of Fame. *(1944)*

David Clayton-Thomas, musician best known as lead singer of Blood, Sweat & Tears, and for writing their hit "Spinning Wheel." *(1941)*

Lewie Steinberg, best known as the original bass guitar player for Booker T. & the M.G.'s; member of the Rock and Roll Hall of Fame. *(1933)*

Mel Tormé, singer-songwriter nicknamed the "Velvet Fog;" composed "The Christmas Song (Chestnuts Roasting on an Open Fire)." *(1908)*

Mel Tormé with Carol Burnett on *The Carol Burnett Show*

Maurice Jarre, composer and conductor who scored films including *Lawrence of Arabia, Doctor Zhivago, A Passage to India, Witness,* and *Ghost. (1924)*

Charles Brown, blues singer whose best known hits include "Driftin' Blues" and "Merry Christmas Baby;" member of the Rock and Roll Hall of Fame. *(1922)*

Dick Haymes, popular male vocalist in the 1940s and early 1950s known for his work with the Andrews Sisters and Bing Crosby; hosted his own radio show for four years. *(1918)*

Ray Charles, singer-songwriter known for the Ray Charles Singers, a regular on Perry Como's television series; not the famous soul singer-songwriter. *(1918)*

Bill Monroe, known as the "father of bluegrass" for his pioneering role in developing that style of music, founded the Blue Grass Boys and the Original Bluegrass Band. *(1911)*

Larry Shields, clarinetist with the Original Dixieland Jazz Band, the first jazz band to record commercially. *(1893)*

Arnold Schoenberg, avant-garde German composer and music theorist known for his modernist atonal compositions; his works were labeled "degenerate music" by the Nazi Party. *(1874)*

Ray Charles (Photo: Capt. Mike)

Bill Monroe with brother Charlie Monroe (1936)

Science and Technology

Leopold Ružička, Croatian scientist who shared the 1939 Nobel Prize for Chemistry for his work on the sex hormones androsterone and testosterone. *(1886)*

Robert Robinson, British scientist who won the 1947 Nobel Prize for Chemistry for his research on anthocyanins and alkaloids. *(1886)*

Oliver Evans, American inventor who designed and built the first fully automated industrial process, the first high-pressure steam engine, the first amphibious vehicle, and the first American automobile. *(1755)*

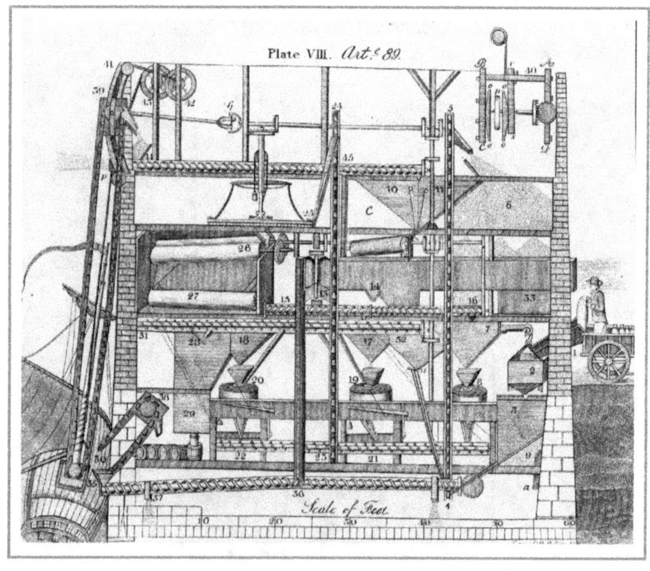

Automated mill for processing grain, designed by **Oliver Evans**.
(Illustration by James Poupard)

Sports and Games

Bernie Williams, center fielder for the New York Yankees for 16 years; five time All-Star and winner of four Gold Glove Awards. Following his baseball career, he became a jazz guitarist nominated in 2009 for a Latin Grammy. *(1968)*

Bernie Williams in 2005 (Photo: Google Man, CC BY-SA 3.0)

Brad Johnson, NFL quarterback who is the first and only player in NFL history to complete a touchdown pass to himself. *(1968)*

Michael Johnson, winner of four Olympic gold medals in sprinting at the 1992, 1996, and 2000 games. *(1967)*

Annie Duke, championship poker player and author of instructional books on the game, as well as a 2005 autobiography *How I Raised, Folded, Bluffed, Flirted, Cursed, and Won Millions at the World Series of Poker.* *(1965)*

Midget Farrelly, won the inaugural World Surfing Championship; member of the Surfing Walk Hall of Fame. *(1944)*

Morris Kirksey, American track and field athlete and rugby player who is one of only four athletes to win gold medals in two different Olympic sports. *(1895)*

Antony Noghès, founder of the Monaco Grand Prix, part of the Triple Crown of Motorsport along with the Indianapolis 500 and Le Mans. *(1890)*

Morris Kirksey

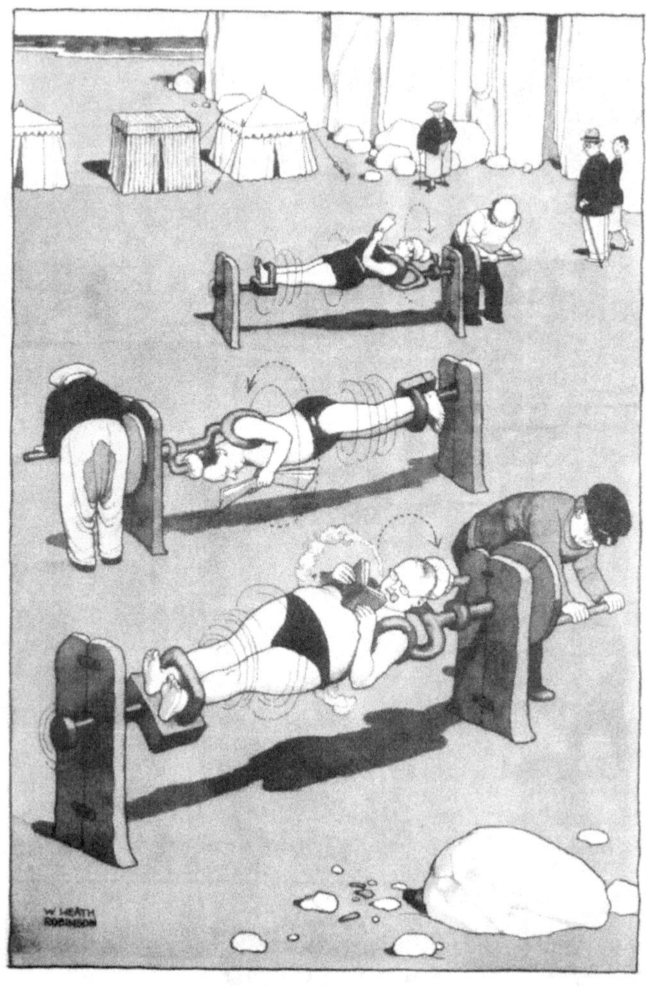

The Sunbathing Wheel   131

"The Sunbathing Wheel," by **Heath Robinson**

Who Died on September 13?

Art and Illustration

George Stanley, Canadian historian who designed the "Maple Leaf" Canadian flag. *(2002)*

The Canadian flag, designed by **George Stanley**

Johnny Craig, comics artist best known for his EC Comics work; member of the Will Eisner Comic Book Hall of Fame. *(2001)*

Reed Crandall, comics artist best known for his association with the EC Comics line, and for his 1940s aviator series *Blackhawk*. Member of the Will Eisner Comic Book Hall of Fame. *(1982)*

Heath Robinson, English cartoonist known for drawing ridiculously complicated machines, known in the UK as "Heath Robinson contraptions." *(1944)*

Business

Mohammed bin Awad bin Laden (محمد بن عوض بن لادن), multi-billionaire who founded the Saudi Binladen Group; father of al-Qaeda leader Osama bin Laden. *(1967)*

Elias Disney, farmer and businessman best known as the father of Walt Disney. *(1941)*

Entertainment

Paul Burke, actor best known for his leading roles in the TV series *Naked City* and *Twelve O'Clock High*. *(2009)*

Joe Pasternak, filmmaker whose best known works include *Destry Rides Again, The Great Caruso, Please Don't Eat the Daisies, Where the Boys Are, The Courtship of Eddie's Father,* and the Elvis Presley vehicles *Girl Happy* and *Spinout*. *(1987)*

Mervyn LeRoy, filmmaker whose best known works include *Little Caesar, Million Dollar Mermaid, Mister Roberts,* and *Gypsy*. *(1987)*

Government and Military

Ann Richards, Texas governor known for her outspoken feminism and her one-liners. *(2006)*

George Wallace, Alabama governor and presidential candidate best known for his pro-segregation and social conservative views and for surviving a 1972 assassination attempt that left him wheelchair-bound. *(1998)*

George Wallace (Photo: *US News & World Report*)

Ambrose Burnside, Union general during the American Civil War, chiefly remembered by his distinctive style of facial hair, which became known as "sideburns" after his last name. *(1881)*

Ambrose Burnside (Photo: Mathew Brady and Levin Handy)

Philip II of Spain, King of Spain during the height of Spain's influence and power; also King of Naples, Sicily, and (as husband to Queen Mary I) King of England and Ireland. *(1598)*

Philip II of Spain, by Titian

Titus, emperor of Rome following the death of his father Vespasian; known for his earlier capture of Jerusalem and destruction of the Second Temple. *(81)*

Literature and Philosophy

Montaigne, philosopher and writer during the French Renaissance; popularized the essay as a literary genre. *(1592)*

Montaigne

Music

Tupak Shakur, rapper and actor who became one of the best-selling music artists of all time; member of the Rock and Roll Hall of Fame. *(1996)*

Leopold Stokowski, classical music conductor best known for appearing in the 1940 Disney film *Fantasia. (1977)*

Science and Medicine

Robert J. Behnke, fisheries biologist known as "The Trout Doctor" for his expertise in the field of salmonid fishes. *(2013)*

Luis E. Miramontes, Mexican chemist known as one of the inventors of the first oral contraceptive pill. *(2004)*

August Krogh, Danish scientist who received the 1920 Nobel Prize in Physiology or Medicine for his discovery of the mechanism of regulation of capillaries in skeletal muscle. *(1949)*

Lili Elbe, Danish transgender woman who was one of the first identifiable recipients of sex reassignment surgery. *(1931)*

Sports

Moses Malone, basketball center named to the Naismith Memorial Basketball Hall of Fame in his first year of eligibility. *(2015)*

Moses Malone (Photo: Cpl. Lameen Witter, USMC)

Erma Bergmann, pitcher with the All-American Girls Professional Baseball League from 1946 through 1951. *(2015)*

Helen Filarski, played in the All-American Girls Professional Baseball League from 1945 to 1950. *(2014)*

Rick Casares, fullback for the Chicago Bears, Washington Redskins, and Miami Dolphins. *(2013)*

Rick Casares

Carl Voss, NHL forward, manager, and coach named to the Hockey Hall of Fame for his contributions to the game. *(1993)*

Quote of the Day

"A little nonsense now and then, is
cherished by the wisest men."

Roald Dahl, novelist
born September 13, 1916

Holidays
Around
the World

September 13

Emperor Marcus Aurelius offers a sacrifice celebrating with the Temple of Jupiter on the Capitoline Hill, Rome, in the background. This is the only existing portrayal of this Roman temple (Photo: Matthias Kabel, CC BY-SA 3.0) — for **Epulum Jovis**

September 13 Events

If you're looking for a reason to take your special day off, you should know that every single day is a holiday somewhere in the world! Here's some of what you can celebrate on September 13!

General Events

Day of the Programmer (international)

Initiated by two Russian programmers and now recognized internationally, the Day of the Programmer is celebrated on the 256th (2^8) day of the year, September 13 in common years and September 12th in leap years.

Día de los Niños Héroes (Mexico)

Six Mexican teenage military cadets.(the Boy Soldiers) died defending Mexico City's Chapultepec Castle from invading US forces on September 13, 1847. The anniversary of their sacrifice is a national holiday in Mexico. *(Illustration page 15.)*

Engineer's Day (Mauritius)

The island nation of Mauritius honors its engineers each September 13.

Epulum Jovis (ancient Rome)

The Epulum Jovis was a ritual feast in honor of the Roman god Jupiter (Jove), celebrated on the Ides of September (September 13). The Roman gods attended the feast in the form of statues; the priests ate the food on their behalf.

Uncle Sam Day (United States)

Established by a joint resolution of Congress in 1989, Uncle Sam Day honors the well-known symbol of America, made famous in a World War I poster by James Montgomery Flagg.

The famous 1917 recruiting poster featuring Uncle Sam, by James Montgomery Flagg — for **Uncle Sam Day**

Friday the Thirteenth

While September 13 doesn't come on Friday every year, sooner or later, every 13th day of the month eventually lands on the dreaded last day of the week.

Friday the 13th is considered an unlucky day in many (but not all) Western nations. Both the number 13 and Friday have a history of being thought unlucky, so when you put the two togethe.... The idea that Friday is unlucky seems to be a maritime superstition — sailors believed it was unlucky to start a voyage on a Friday.

(Photo: W. J. Pilsak, CC BY-SA 3.0)

As far as the number 13 goes, there are a number of theories.One theory is that it refers to the 13 people around the table at the Last Supper, one of whom (Judas) would shortly betray Jesus. Others point out that on Friday, October 13, 1307, the Knights Templar were arrested, and many of them were later tortured and killed. In Norse mythology, Loki becomes the 13th guest when he crashes a party in Valhalla; the fallout results in the death of Baldur.

Fear of the number thirteen is common enough that a psychological condition, *triskaidekaphobia*, is named for it! (Fear of Friday the 13th is *paraskevidekatriaphobi*a.)

According to some researchers, between 17 and 21 million people in the US alone are bothered by Friday 13th. Fear of thirteen is so common that many tall buildings skip 13 when numbering floors — over 80 percent of high-rise buildings in the US alone! Many hotels, hospitals, and airports don't have rooms or gates numbered 13 either.

Perhaps some of the bad luck associated with Friday 13th is self-inflicted. Fewer people drive on Friday 13th, but there are more accidents.

In Spanish-speaking countries, as well as in Greece, they worry about Tuesday 13th (*martes trece*) instead —though either way, January 13 qualifies. In Italy, though, 13 is a lucky number — but watch out for Friday the 17th!

In most of Asia, the number four is considered unlucky — the Chinese words for "four" and "death" are similar. Buildings in Asia may have a 13th floor, but often don't have a 4th floor.

Miss Rose Cade, "Queen of the Lemons," was nominated to be southern California's "Swat the Jinx" girl in 1920 — for **Friday the Thirteenth**

Food Days

In the United States, almost every day of the year is dedicated to a particular food. (Some other countries also have official food days, but only in America is there one every single day!) Sponsored by manufacturers, retailers, farmers, or simply fans, these days are often proclaimed by the President, Congress, state governors, or mayors. Given that there are more different foods than days of the year, some days honor more than one kind of food!

In the US, September 13 is **National Peanut Day.** Peanuts, of course, are actually legumes rather than nuts, but lots of people are nuts for peanuts.

George Washington Carver — for **National Peanut Day**

The peanut originated in northwestern Argentina and southeastern Bolivia some 7,600 years ago, and spread throughout South America. With the European arrival, peanuts spread throughout the world and today Asia produces the most peanuts.

In the Americas, peanut growing today takes place primarily in North America. At first, peanuts were grown for animal feed, but in the late 19th century, the US Department of Agriculture started encouraging peanuts for human consumption. Botanist and inventor George Washington Carver created hundreds of recipes for peanuts.

Peanut products include peanut oil, peanut flower, and peanut butter. Around the world, peanuts are boiled, roasted, sauced, and made into stews and soups.They're used in candies, cakes, cookies, and can even be made into milk.

Although peanut allergies can be deadly, the humble peanut is a staple food around the world, and is even used to combat malnutrition.

Roasted Peanuts (Photo: Geographer, CC BY-SA 2.5) — for **National Peanut Day**

In most places, Chocolate Day is celebrated on July 7, but the US National Confectioners Association lists September 13 as **International Chocolate Day**. There are other days for milk chocolate, white chocolate, and cocoa, in case you're in the mood for something to mix with your peanut butter.

An assortment of chocolates (Photo: Arnaud25, CC BY-SA 4.0) — for **International Chocolate Day**

Food Months

The entire month of September is used to celebrate numerous foods. Here's a list of what to eat this month!

- Bourbon Heritage Month
- California Wine Month

A glass and bottle of bourbon, for **Bourbon Heritage Month**
(Photo: Dirk Ingo Franke, CC BY-SA 4.0)

- National Chicken Month
- National Honey Month
- National Mushroom Month
- National Papaya Month
- National Potato Month
- National Rice Month
- National Whole Grains Month
- National Wild Rice Month

Religious Feast Days and Holidays

Saint Days

Each day in the year is considered a feast day for one or more saints. They are somewhat different in western Christianity (Catholicism and many forms of Protestantism) and in eastern (Orthodox) Christianity.

In *Western Christianity*, September 13 is the feast day of Saints Aimé, Ame, Eulogius of Alexandria, John Chrysostom, Marcellinus of Carthage, Maurille of Angers, Nectarius of Autun, Venerius the Hermit, and Wilfrida of Wilton.

In *Eastern Orthodox Christianity*, it is also the commemoration of Saints Aristides the Athenian, Philip, Litorius, Columbinus, Barsenorius, Hedwig, John of Prislop, Cornelius of Padan-Olonets, and Meletius I Pegas,. (These saints are honored on August 31 by "Old Calendrists[†].")

Non-Gregorian Religious Events

Not every culture uses the familiar Gregorian calendar, so some events not only shift within a range of a few days depending on the year, but may even migrate through the months. Here is a selection of events around the world that sometimes take place on September 13.

- Aadi Perukku (Tamil calendar, Hinduism)
- Anant Chaturdashi (Hindus and Jains)
- Binara Poya (Buddhism)

[†] "Old Calendrists" use the older Julian calendar for liturgical purposes rather than the modern Gregorian one. See "What Day of the Week is September 13?"for the differences between the Julian and Gregorian calendars.

- Chaturmas (Hindu calendar, also observed in Jainism, Buddhism)
- Gai Jatra (Nepali calendar)
- Ghanta Karna (Nepali calendar)
- Jhulan Purnima (Hindu calendar)
- Kumbh Mela (Hindu calendar)
- Nag Panchami (Hindu calendar)
- Onam (Malayalam Calendar, Hinduism)
- Pitru Paksha (Hinduism)
- Raksha Bandhan (Hindu calendar)
- Rosh Hashanah LaBehema (Judaism)
- Shravana Putrada Ekadashi (Hindu calendar)
- Teejdi 3rd day of Raksha Bandhan (Hindu calendar)
- Varalakshmi Vratam (Hindu calendar)
- Vassa (Theravada Buddhism)

Saint John Chrysostom, by Petro Orrente (Prado Museum)

Honorary Months and Moveable Celebrations

Presidents, Congresses, and nations around the world issue proclamations recognizing particular months to honor certain causes. If not otherwise specified, all months are US. Here are some honorary designations for August.

- Baby Safety Month
- Be Kind to Editors and Writers Month
- Children's Good Manners Month
- College Savings Month
- Happy Cat Month
- International Square Dancing Month
- National Preparedness Month
- National Recovery Month
- National Service Dog Month
- National Yoga Month
- Pain Awareness Month
- Responsible Dog Ownership Month

Moveable and Multi-Day Events

Some events take place over a specific week or time period. Some events occur on different days each year (such as "fourth Saturday of a month"). These events sometimes take place on or include September 13. All are US unless otherwise specified.

Second Saturday

- Day of the Workers in the Oil, Gas, Power, and Geological Industry (Turkmenistan)

- National Iguana Awareness Day
- Prairie Day

An iguana in the Galapagos (Photo: Simon Matzinger, CC BY-SA 4.0) — for **National Iguana Awareness Day**

Second Sunday

- Auditor's Day (Scientology)
- Father's Day (Latvia)
- National Grandparent's Day (Canada, Estonia) *(Photo next page)*
- National Pet Memorial Day
- Tanker's Day (Russia)

First Sunday after the first Monday

- National Grandparent's Day (United States)

Nearest Weekday to September 12

- Saragarhi Day (Sikhism)

Visiting Grandmother, Felix Schlesinger — for **National Granparent's Day**

Just for Fun

Anybody can make up a holiday, and many people do! While none of these are officially recognized and some may come and go, here are a few more holidays for September 13.

- International Drive Your Studebaker Day (2nd Saturday)
- Kids Take Over the Kitchen Day
- National Hollerin' Day (2nd Saturday)
- Roald Dahl Day (Africa, the United Kingdom, and Latin America)
- Scooby-Doo Day

A 1961 Studebaker Hawk in the Netherlands (Photo: Alf van Beem) — for **International Drive Your Studebaker Day**

Quote of the Day

"O sweet September, thy first breezes bring
The dry leaf's rustle and the squirrel's laughter,
The cool fresh air whence health and vigor spring
And promise of exceeding joy hereafter."

George Arnold, *September Days*

About
the
Month
of
September

"September," by Eugène Grasset

September: The Ninth Month

The morrow was a bright September morn;
The earth was beautiful as if new-born;
There was that nameless splendor everywhere,
That wild exhilaration in the air,
Which makes the passers in the city street
Congratulate each other as they meet.

Henry Wadsworth Longfellow, "Tales of a Wayside Inn"

In Latin, *septem* means "seven," so it may seem strange that September is actually the *ninth* month of the year. The original Roman calendar, on which ours is based, started in March, making September indeed the seventh month. No one is completely sure when the start of the year was moved to January, but the traditional name of September stuck.

Romans also associated September with the god Vulcan, and thus expected the month to have fires, volcanic eruptions, and earthquakes.

In the northern hemisphere, September marks the beginning of meteorological autumn. In the southern hemisphere, September is the seasonal equivalent of March, the beginning of spring.

September and December always begin on the same day of the week. However, no other month in the same year will end on the same day of the week as September.

For countries that switched from the Julian to the Gregorian calendars in 1752, the date jumped from September 2 to September 14, meaning that September 3 through 13 don't exist in that year.

September in Other Cultures

In Old English, the month of September was known as *Hāligmōnaþ*. Anglo-Saxons called it *Gerst monath* (Barley month) celebrating the barley harvest that would shortly be turned into beer.

In Finland, it is *syyskuu*, in Poland *wrzesień*, and in Greece *Σεπτέμβριος*. The Russians call the month *сентябрь*.

While both the Hebrew and Arabic cultures have their own calendar system, the Hebrew word for "September" is ספטמבר and in Arabic it's سبتمب.

The Azerbaijani call the month *Sentyabr*.

In Hindi, the month of "sitambar" is written सतिबर.

In both China and Japan, it's known as 九月, 구월 in Korea, and 腩尬 in Vietnam.

Afternoon in September, Frank Weston Benson

September Symbols

Birthstone: Sapphire, representing clear thinking.

Star sapphire

Birth Flowers: Forget-me-not, morning glory, and aster.

Forget-me-not (*moyosotis azorica*)

September Sayings and Superstitions

Here are some wedding sayings and superstitions associated with the month of September.

- "Marry in September's shrine, your living with be rich and fine."
- "A September bride will be discreet, affable, and much liked."
- "Married in September's golden glow / Smooth and serene your life will go."

As for which day of the week, that's easy.

Monday for health, Tuesday for wealth,
Wednesday best of all, Thursday for losses,
Friday for crosses, Saturday for no luck at all.

A Regency wedding proposal

September, by Joachim von Sandrart

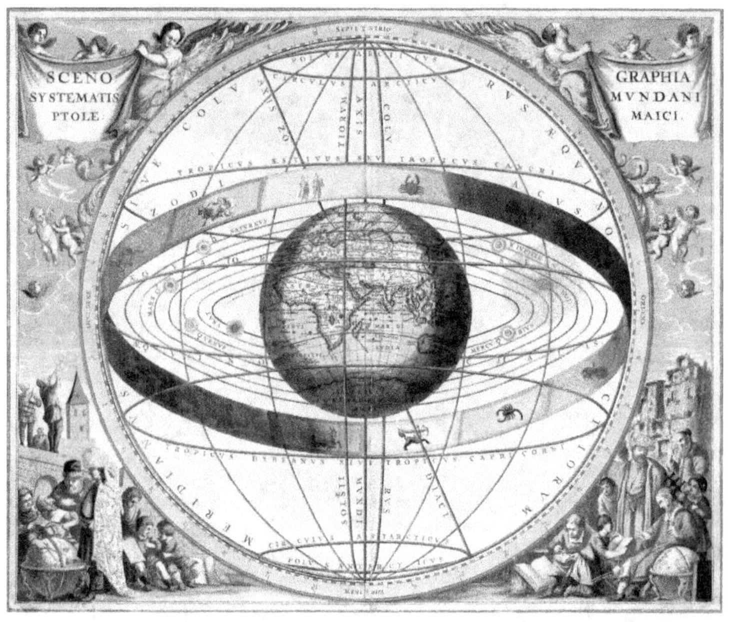

Scenography of the Ptolemaic Cosmography, by Johannes van Loon, based on Andreas Cellarius's *Harmonia Macrocosmica*, 1660

September 13 Zodiac Signs

From the perspective of someone on Earth, the Sun appears to move through the sky throughout the year, along a path astronomers call the *ecliptic plane*. The ecliptic plane is divided into twelve constellations, known as the zodiac, based on traditionally observed patterns of stars. On your birthday, you can't see your constellation, because it's in the daytime sky.

The zodiac was first developed by Babylonian astronomers about 2,500 years ago. Because they were unaware that the Earth wobbles like a spinning top (known as *precession*), they didn't make allowance for the fact that the Sun's path through the zodiac changes over time.

That means there are now two sets of dates for your birth sign. The *tropical dates* are the original Babylonian dates; the *sidereal dates* tell you where the Sun actually appears as it moves along its annual path.

For September 13, the tropical sign is **Virgo** and the sidereal sign is **Leo.**

Virgo

Tropical August 23 to September 23
Sidereal September 16 to October 15

The constellation of Virgo was originally associated with the grain harvest and symbolized fertility. The Greeks and Romans saw Virgo as Demeter or Ceres, the goddess of agriculture. In art, Virgo is often represented as carrying two sheaves of wheat. In the Middle Ages, Virgo was also sometimes connected to the Virgin Mary.

In astrology, Virgos are associated with being observant, helpful, and reliable, but can be perceived as inflexible and cold. They are supposed to be compatible with Taurus, Cancer, and Capricorn, but not with Gemini, Libra, or Aries.

Leo

Tropical July 23 to August 22
Sidereal August 16 to September 15

Leo is one of the earliest recognizable constellations, with its stars forming a sickle or backward question mark. The Mesopotamians, the Persians, the Jews, and the Indians all had a name for the constellation that meant "lion." In Greek mythology, the Nemean lion was impervious to any weapons, but the hero Hercules nevertheless defeated it.

In astrology, Leo is a fire sign, suggesting that Leos are strong-willed and passionate. Leos are supposed to be compatible with Aquarius, Aries, and Sagittarius, but not with Gemini, Capricorn, or Pisces.

Illustration by Edward Penfield

What Day of the Week is September 13?

On what day of the week does September 13 fall?

Surprisingly, this isn't an easy question. Because the calendar year is 365 days long (366 in leap years), it doesn't divide evenly by the seven days of the week.

Also, the Earth goes around the Sun in about 365-1/4 days, so a calendar tends to drift over time. That's why the same date falls on different weekdays in different years.

This is made even more complicated by a change in calendars that took place in 1582. Our modern calendar has its roots in ancient Rome, in a calendar reform conducted by Julius Caesar. Caesar commissioned mathematicians to attack the problem, and they came up with the idea of leap years, and thus standardized the calendar for centuries to come. This was called the Julian calendar.

Over time, however, the small errors in Caesar's calculation compounded. That's why Pope Gregory XIII commissioned the Gregorian calendar, used in most of the world today. Some countries converted in 1582, when the calendar was first developed; some converted later; other still haven't changed.

Gregorian and Julian aren't the only types of calendars. The Hebrew year, the Islamic year, and many other calendars are used in different parts of the world and among different people.

You can convert Gregorian dates to other calendars, including the Hebrew calendar, the Islamic calendar, and even the Mayan calendar by visiting the Fourmilab Calendar Converter at http://www.fourmilab.ch/documents/calendar/.

Chinese calendar systems are quite complex and have changed several times; a full discussion is far beyond the scope of this book. If you're interested, you can find information here: http://www.hermetic.ch/cal_stud/chinese_cal.htm.

On Names and Dates

Historians use "CE" (Common Era) and "BCE" (Before the Common Era) instead of the more common "AD" (Anno Domini, or Year of Our Lord) and "BC" (Before Christ), reflecting the fact that the year-numbering system established by the Gregorian calendar is used throughout the world in many countries not culturally Christian.

The CE/BCE designation dates back to at least 1708, and has been adopted as a standard by the United Nations and the Universal Postal Union. Because this series of books covers events and people of all nations and cultures, we use the CE/BCE terms.

The abbreviation "O.S." ("Old Style") and "N.S." ("New Style") on some dates refers to the fact that the Russian Empire (in particular) did not switch from the Julian to the Gregorian calendar at the same time as the rest of Europe, and therefore some figures and events have two dates.

Also, in the Julian calendar in England in the 16th century, the year began on March 25 rather than January 1. To avoid confusion with Gregorian dates, dates between January and March were often written using both years.

People and events whose original names are not in the Western alphabet have their native names (where possible) in the appropriate script shown in parenthesis. If you are using an e-reader to access an electronic version of this book, all characters don't always display on all devices.

A 50-year brass perpetual calendar.

Quote of the Day

"Time is an illusion, lunchtime doubly so."

Douglas Adams,
from *The Hitchhiker's Guide to the Galaxy*

85

Cartoon by John T. McCutcheon

Copyright, Credit, and Contact

Follow Us

Our blog "This Day in History" (http://
timespinnerpress.com/this-day-in-history/) features short
articles on events and people associated with each day, and
updates several times each week. Also subscribe to the
"Quote of the Day" at http://timespinnerpress.com/quote-
of-the-day/. You can get daily links by following us on
Facebook at TimespinnerPress, or on Twitter as
@sidewisethinker.

Contact Us

Find an error or a format problem? Want information about
the series, about us, or about when the volume for your
special day might be available? Please email us at
editor@timespinnerpress.com. (We also take requests if your
special day isn't yet complete. Please give us at least six
weeks' notice if possible.)

Sources

We owe a great debt to Wikipedia, which is our first stop for
research. We attempt to make independent confirmation of
all important dates and facts through a variety of other
sources.

Other sources we frequently use include the Library of
Congress; "on this day" listings from *Encyclopedia Britannica*,
the *New York Times*, and the BBC; Omniglot for the names of
months in other languages; *Chase's Calendar of Events*; and, of
course, the always essential Google.

All art and photographs are either in the public domain, used under a Creative Commons license, or with a "fair use" justification, and most frequently come from Wikimedia Commons and the Library of Congress Prints and Photographs Division.

Attribution is provided where possible, or as requested by the copyright owner, or when there is particular historical significance, listed below. For information about any particular illustration or photograph, please contact us.

Credits

1. The cover photograph of Michelangelo's *David* was taken in 2008 by Jörg Bittner Unna, who holds the copyright. It is used here under CC BY-SA 3.0.

2. The illustration of the month of September used on the back cover is from the French Gothic illuminated manuscript *Les Très Riches Heures du duc de Berry* by the Limbourg Brothers, Jean Colombe, and an intermediate painter whose name is lost to history. It is in the public domain because its copyright has expired.

3. The box graphic used on the first page is from a 1916 pamphlet entitled "Divorce versus Democracy" authored by G. K. Chesterton, originally published in London by the Society of St. Peter and St. Paul. It is in the public domain in the US because it was published prior to 1923, and is in the public domain in all countries (including the country of origin) in which the copyright time is the author's life plus 70 years or less.

4. The graphic design for the section pages in this book is from a design originally created for a pharmacy label. It is courtesy of Wellcome Images (ICV No 11073, photo V0010813), and is used here under CC BY-SA 4.0.

5. The painting *September* is from the *Brevarium Grimani*, circa 1510, and is in the public domain because its copyright has expired.

6. The 2014 photograph of *David* was taken by Korido, who holds the copyright. It is used here under CC BY-SA 4.0.

7. The 1912 painting *By Dawn's Early Light* by Edward Percy Moran is in the public domain because its copyright has expired.

8.   The 1964 photograph of the Star-Spangled Banner flag is courtesy Smithsonian Institution Archives (SIA), who have determined that there are no known copyright restrictions on the use of this image.

9.   The 16th century portrait of John Calvin, incorrectly credited to Hans Holbein the Younger, is in the public domain because its copyright has expired.

10. The circa 1847 Currier & Ives print of the Military College of Chapultepec is in the public domain because its copyright has expired. It is available from the Library of Congress Prints and Photographs Division, digital ID cph.3g06246.

11. The 1962 photograph "Integration at Ole Miss" was taken by *US News & World Report* staff photographer Marion S. Trikosko. It is in the public domain as part of the *US News & World Report* Magazine Collection donated to the Library of Congress (digital ID ppmsca. 04292). Per the deed of gift, *U.S. News & World Report* dedicated to the public all rights it held for the photographs in this collection upon its donation to the Library.

12. The 1873 photograph of Henry Bliss is in the public domain because its copyright has expired.

13. The 1943 photograph of Senator Margaret Chase Smith is in the public domain because it was first published in the United States between 1923 and 1977 without a copyright notice. It is from the Library of Congress, digital ID cph.3a42977.

14. The photograph of General John J. Pershing is by George Grantham Bain/Bain News Service. It is part of the George Grantham Bain Collection donated to the Library of Congress (digital ID ggbain. 21134). According to the Library, there are no known restrictions on the use of photographs from this collection.

15. The 1920s publicity photograph of Claudette Colbert is in the public domain because it was first published in the United States between 1923 and 1977 without a copyright notice. Traditionally, publicity photographs are not copyrighted because of the way in which they are intended to be used.

16. The 1973 "LOVE" stamp is in the public domain as a work created by an employee of the US government as part of that person's official duties. (This applies to stamps published prior to 1978.)

17. The 1905 photograph of Milton S. Hershey is in the public domain because its copyright has expired.

18. The 1969 publicity photograph from *Mission: Impossible* is in the public domain because it was first published in the United States between 1923 and 1977 without a copyright notice.

19. The 1964 screenshot from the trailer for the film *Mary Poppins* is in the public domain because it was first published in the United States between 1923 and 1977 without a copyright notice. Although the motion picture itself is copyrighted, traditionally trailers were not copyrighted because of the way in which they are intended to be used.

20. The 1930s publicity photograph of Mae Questel is in the public domain because it was first published in the United States between 1923 and 1977 without a copyright notice.

21. The painting *Portrait of a Gentleman (Cesare Borgia)* by Altobello Melone was created between 1500 and 1524, and is in the public domain because its copyright has expired. It is in the collection of the Accademia Carrara, Bergamo, Italy.

22. The photograph of Roald Dahl and Patricia Neal is by Carl Van Vechten. It is part of the Carl Van Vechten Collection donated to the Library of Congress (reproduction number LC-USZ62-103964 DLC). According to the Library, there are no known restrictions on the use of photographs from this collection.

23. The 1969 publicity photograph from *The Carol Burnett Show* is in the public domain because it was first published in the United States between 1923 and 1977 without a copyright notice.

24. The 1975 photograph of Ray Charles is copyright © Captain Mike1, and is used here under CC BY-SA 4.0.

25. The 1936 photograph of the Monroe Brothers by Norran Lamberson is in the public domain in Germany, its country of origin, because its copyright has expired.

26. The 1795 illustration of an automated mill is by James Poupard, and first appeared in Oliver Evans' book *The Young Mill-Wright and Miller's Guide*. It is in the public domain because its copyright has expired.

27. The 2005 photograph of Bernie Williams is copyright © by Google man (at) en.wikipedia, and is used here under CC BY-SA 3.0.

28. The 1920 photograph of Morris Kirksey is from the Bibliothèque nationale de France, who placed the work in the public domain under CC0 1.0.

29. "The Sunbathing Wheel" by William Heath Robinson first appeared in the 1973 book *Heath Robinson Inventions*. It is in the public domain in the UK, its country of origin, and in other areas where the copyright term is the author's life plus 70 years or fewer. (Robinson died in 1944.)

30. The flag of Canada is not an object of copyright.

31. The 1968 photograph of George Wallace was taken by a *US News & World Report* staff photographer. It is in the public domain as part of the *US News & World Report* Magazine Collection donated to the Library of Congress (digital ID ppmsca.19605). Per the deed of gift, *U.S. News & World Report* dedicated to the public all rights it held for the photographs in this collection upon its donation to the Library.

32. The photograph of Ambrose Burnside was taken by Mathew Brady and Levin Handy between 1865 and 1880, and is in the public domain because its copyright has expired. It is from the Brady-Handy Photo Collection at the Library of Congress (digital ID cwpbh.04980).

33. The portrait of Philip II of Spain by Titian was painted between 1545 and 1556 and is in the public domain because its copyright has expired. It is in the collection of the Cincinnati Art Museum.

34. The illustration of Montaigne is in the public domain because its copyright has expired.

35. The 2005 photograph of Moses Malone was taken by US Marine Cpl. Lameen Witter. It is in the public domain as a work created by an employee of the US government as part of that person's official duties.

36. The 1953 photograph of Rick Casares is in the public domain because it was first published in the United States between 1923 and 1977 without a copyright notice.

37. The 2009 photograph of the bas-relief of Marcus Aurelius is copyright © Matthias Kabel, and is used here under CC BY-SA 3.0.

38. The 1917 "Uncle Sam" recruiting poster by James Montgomery Flagg is in the public domain as a work created by an employee of the US government as part of that person's official duties. Courtesy Library of Congress Prints and Photographs Division (digital ID ppmsca.50554).

39. The photograph of a calendar showing Friday the 13th was taken by W. J. Pilsak, who holds the copyright, and is used here under CC BY-SA 3.0.

40. The 1920 photograph of Miss Rose Cade is from the Keystone View Company. It is in the public domain because its copyright has expired.

41. The 2007 photograph of two roasted peanuts is copyrighted © by Geographer (at) en.wikipedia, and is used here under CC BY-SA 2.5.

42. The 1910 photograph of George Washington Carver is from the Tuskegee University Archives and Museum. It is in the public domain because its copyright has expired.

43. The 2014 photograph of chocolates is copyright © Arnaud 25, and is used here under CC BY-SA 4.0.

44. The 2015 photograph of bourbon is copyright © Dirk Ingo Franke, and is used here under CC BY-SA 4.0.

45. The 17th century painting *San Juan Crisóstomo* by Pedro Orrente is in the public domain because its copyright has expired. It is in the Museo del Prado, Madrid, accession number P07640.

46. The 2014 photograph of a Galapagos land iguana is copyright © Simon Matzinger. It is used here under CC BY-SA 4.0.

47. The painting *Bei Großmutter* by Felix Schlesinger was created prior to 1910 and is in the public domain because its copyright has expired.

48. The 2009 photograph of a Studebaker Hawk is by Alf van Beem, who released the image into the public domain under CC0 1.0.

49. The 1896 illustration *September* by Eugène Grasset is in the public domain because its copyright has expired.

50. The 1913 painting *Afternoon in September* by Frank Weston Benson is in the public domain because its copyright has expired. It is in the collection of the National History Museum of Los Angeles County.

51. The photograph of a star sapphire was released into the public domain by its author, Mitchell Gore.

52. The chromolithograph of a forget-me-not is by Louis-Aristide Léon Constans and originally appeared in the 1852-1853 edition of Paxton's Flower Garden. It is in the public domain because its copyright has expired.

53. The painting *September* by Joachim von Sandrart is in the public domain because its copyright has expired. The original can be found in the Staatsgalerie im Neuen Schloss, Schleißheim, Germany.

54. The celestial sphere is from *Scenography of the Ptolemaic Cosmography*, by Johannes van Loon, based on Andreas Cellarius's *Harmonia Macrocosmica*, 1660. It is in the public domain because its copyright has expired.

55. The 1906 automobile calendar is by Edward Penfield, and is in the collection of the Library of Congress Prints and Photographs Division. It is in the public domain because its copyright has expired.

56. The 50-year perpetual calendar photograph is in the public domain.

57. The cartoon by John T. McCutcheon is from his 1905 collection *The Mysterious Stranger and Other Cartoons by John T. McCutcheon*. It is in the public domain because its copyright has expired.

58. The detail from the painting *Augsburg Labours of the Months: Autumn*, by Jörg Breu the Elder was created prior to 1550, and is in the public domain because its copyright has expired. The painting is in the Deutches Historisches Museum, Berlin.

59. The painting *September* by Hans Thoma is from his book *Festkalender*. It is in the public domain because its copyright has expired.

License Description and Terms

Aside from material purely in the public domain, photographs and other material in this book are used under specific licenses permitting free use, usually with an attribution requirement. For full text and terms of these licenses, click or enter the appropriate links below. If you believe there is an error in the copyright status or attribution of any of these images, please email us.

- Creative Commons Attribution 2.0 Generic (CC-BY 2.0): http:// creativecommons.org/licenses/by/2.0/deed.en
- Creative Commons Attribution-Share Alike 3.0 Generic (CC-BY-SA 3.0): http://creativecommons.org/licenses/by-sa/3.0/
- Creative Commons Attribution-Share Alike 2.5 Generic (CC-BY-SA 2.5): http://creativecommons.org/licenses/by-sa/2.5/deed.en
- Creative Commons Attribution-Share Alike 2.0 Generic (CC-BY-SA 2.0): http://creativecommons.org/licenses/by/2.0/deed.en
- Creative Commons Attribution-Share Alike 1.0 Generic (CC-BY-SA 1.0): http://creativecommons.org/licenses/by-sa/1.0/deed.en
- CC0 1.0 Universal (CC0 1.0) Public Domain Dedication (CC0 1.0) http://creativecommons.org/publicdomain/zero/1.0/deed.en
- GNU Free Documentation License (GFDL): http:// en.wikipedia.org/wiki/ Wikipedia:Text_of_the_GNU_Free_Documentation_License
- License Art Libre (Free Art License): http://artlibre.org

"September," detail from *Augsburg Labours of the Months: Autumn*, by Jörg Breu the Elder (Courtesy Deutches Historisches Museum, Berlin)

Other Books from Timespinner Press

Timespinner
Press

The Story of a Special Day

Michael Dobson

A series of (eventually) 366 volumes covering everything that happened on your special day! Events, births, deaths, quotes, holidays, and much more. It's like a birthday card they'll never throw away!

US$7.95 print/US$2.99 ebook.

From Plassey to Pakistan

Humayun Mirza

The history of British Colonial India and the formation of Pakistan from the unique perspective of the son of Pakistan's first president and last of the royal line of Bengal, Bihar, and Orissa! This unique historical document tells the inside story of this distinguished family, including the detailed story of the coup that toppled his father from power!

US$27.95 print

A Whole New Navy: America's War in the Pacific

Miles Durr

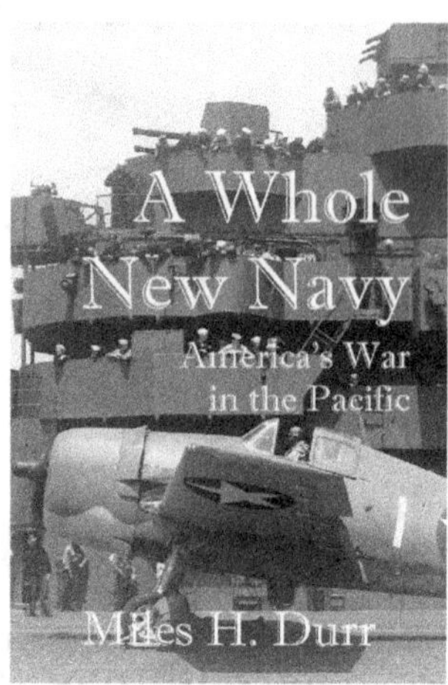

The most comprehensive and detailed description of America's naval war in the Pacific ever—every battle, every ship, every task force and every task group from Pearl Harbor through the Japanese surrender! A must-have for the collection of every World War II buff!

US$29.95 print

Improbable History: The Weird, the Obscure, and the Strangely Important

edited by Michael Dobson

From the birth of Western civilization to the rescue of Apollo 13, from the Leaning Tower of Pisa to Florence's Duomo, history has often turned on small, improbable details. Whatever happened to the ancient Samaritan people? Why did a fortuitous rainstorm allow the British to conquer India? How did an air raid in Italy lead to the development of chemotherapy? What happened when Albert Einstein met Adolf Hitler on the streets of Berlin? How did the Japanese manage to attack the US mainland using balloons? A cast of award-winning writers tackle some of the strangest tales in history!

US$19.95 print

The Letters of William Philip Schwartz 1842-1855

edited by John F. Schwartz

The 19th century soldier and adventurer William Philip Schwartz wrote a series of vivid and detailed letters chronicling his adventures in the Indian Wars, the Mexican-American War, the Gold Rush, and his term as Marine sergeant aboard the USS Constellation. A pioneer in photography, he took *the first known war photographs*. An unforgettable first-hand look into life in the 19th century!

US$17.95 print

Watergate Considered as an Organization Chart of Semi-Precious Stones (and other essays)

by Michael Dobson

In this light-hearted yet insightful tour through the Nixon White House, the Committee to Re-Elect the President, and the various investigative committees, you'll meet fascinating characters from Richard Nixon himself to such lieutenants as a G. Gordon Liddy and John Dean. You'll gain insights into the origin of the scandal, the motives of the players, and how the situation spiraled so badly out of control.

US$9.95 print/US$3.99 ebook

September, by Hans Thoma

9 781979 729871